# Official Soccer Rules Illustrated

## A Quick Reference
## for All Coaches, Players, and Fans

Stanley Lover

Foreword by
Joseph S. Blatter
FIFA President

## TRIUMPH
### BOOKS

## ALSO BY STANLEY LOVER

Soccer Rules Explained
Soccer Laws Illustrated
Soccer Match Control
Soccer Judge
Soccer and Its Rules
Illustrated Soccer Quiz Book
Fair Play Guide
You Are the Ref
Play On!
Masterclass for Soccer Officials
Chronicles of a Timid Lover (autobiography)

This book is available in quantity at special discounts for your group or organization. For further information, contact:

Triumph Books
542 South Dearborn Street
Suite 750
Chicago, Illinois 60605
(312) 939-3330
Fax (312) 663-3557
www.triumphbooks.com

Printed in U.S.A.
ISBN: 978-1-60078-282-4

Design by Amy Carter

Photos courtesy of Getty Images unless otherwise indicated
Illustrations copyright © Stanley Lover

# CONTENTS

# SOCCER — "THE PEOPLE'S GAME"

Soccer has been described as "The People's Game" because it appeals to millions bound together in a world soccer family. It is a joy to play because each player can express personal skills in an exciting sport. It is a joy to watch because the ball is always visible and the play easy to follow.

Soccer is at its best when a game flows from goal to goal and when players display their skills in a spirit of fair play, respecting opponents, officials, and faithful supporters while creating a pleasurable experience.

Making the most of each soccer game requires a basic knowledge of the rules. Players need to know what is fair and unfair to avoid offenses that stop the play, give the ball to the opponents, and frustrate their skills' potential. Coaches and club officials need to know enough to set correct discipline on and off the field. For parents and friends of soccer, a basic knowledge will help them understand and enjoy "The People's Game" better.

The purpose of this book is to provide a visual link between the legalistic text of the official rules and the excitement of actual play.

All rules and interpretations quoted here follow the worldwide FIFA pattern. U.S. college and high school games are allowed minor variations.

# FOREWORD

Over the years, soccer has carved itself a very distinct place in political, cultural, economic, and social life. This was highlighted once again at the 2006 FIFA World Cup Germany™, where millions witnessed soccer as an extravaganza of intense excitement, profound emotion, and heartbreaking drama. Above all, it showed soccer as a powerful unifying force in a divided world.

To preserve the integrity of our sport, we are alert to any attempts to unduly influence results. On the field, our match officials are charged with the task of applying the 17 Laws of the Game with firmness and consistency to ensure the future success of soccer. It is a simple and universal game, and we want to keep it that way. We constantly uphold referees' decisions relating to play even when they sometimes provoke heated debate—for instance, in the case of a close offside call or an incident where the ball goes over the goal line.

Mistakes do occur and are a part of the game. They represent the human element, an emotional factor contributing to the game's attraction. However, we strive to keep mistakes to an acceptable minimum by encouraging the use of professional referees where feasible and showing ever more attention to the training of all match officials in the FIFA family of soccer nations. They are, after all, an integral part of our fascinating game.

I welcome publications such as this, conceived by an acknowledged expert on the game and its rules. The many dynamic illustrations present the essential points of each rule with simplicity, clarity, and authority. Earlier editions have become textbooks worldwide, published in several languages. This new version includes an interesting Soccer IQ test that will entertain and add to your knowledge of the rules of the game.

**—Joseph S. Blatter**
*FIFA President*

# PREFACE

Today's world is a global village, and the beautiful game with a round ball has become the universal language that binds different cultures and nationalities together in an atmosphere of sporting passion. This language is spoken with different dialects and its name may sound different—football, futbol, calcio, or coccer, for example—but no matter how you describe it, it is the world's game. Part of its beauty is that it is played to one set of laws that are universal, designed to keep the game simple and entertaining for the players and fans alike.

The laws and their interpretations are fully understood by referees. They are the guardians of the beautiful game in every match, charged with keeping our sport fair and enjoyable for millions of players and followers.

This book contains essential knowledge of the game and its laws in an easy format to help referees in their task and all members of the soccer family who want to understand the game better.

**—Esfandiar Baharmast**

*U.S. Soccer Director of Advanced and International Referee Development. FIFA Instructor. Achieved personal fame and high respect for U.S. soccer officials at the 1998 FIFA World Cup in France.*

Soccer has been played in its present form since 1863, but the basic principles have hardly changed. Modern soccer rules have adapted to faster pace, higher skills, and advancing technology, but, although players and spectators have a general grasp of their purpose, a mistaken interpretation can provoke unjust criticism of referees' decisions. A better understanding of their application adds to the pleasures of the game.

Referees study hard to apply the spirit, as well as the letter, of the rules to ensure games are played in a sporting climate. This book helps toward a better appreciation of the game and what all soccer people can do to keep it a clean and healthy sport.

**—Ken Aston, M.B.E.**

*International Referee, FIFA Administrator, and Member, International Football Association Board. Honored by the Queen of England for exceptional services to U.S. Soccer. Legendary counselor with the American Youth Soccer Organization.*

# THE SPIRIT OF THE GAME—FAIR PLAY

Soccer is more than a simple game. It is an emotional experience.

The mechanics of play amount to the movement of a ball about the size of a man's head between two targets set some distance apart. But, in the course of just one game, the whole range of human emotions from the depths of despair to utter joy can be touched in the hearts of those who play or watch.

Somewhere in these emotions lies the key to the Spirit of the Game, a term often mentioned but rarely defined. To merely present in these pages a series of illustrations of the written rules, without considering the spirit in which they are intended to be applied, would offer an unfinished story.

The spirit in which the game should be played was considered more important than the written rule by the nineteenth-century founders of the game. A few rules—or Laws, as they were styled—were set down to regulate the physical play, but not a word was included on the principles or ethics to be observed. In those days, it was not necessary to write down a code of conduct. After all, the game as we know it today was devised by intelligent, respected men steeped in the codes of ethics and gentlemanly conduct imposed by the strict era of Queen Victoria of England.

Much wisdom was included in those few early rules, as is evidenced by the fact that the game has remained practically unchanged for more than 140 years. Those early and subsequent legislators have carefully guarded the inner soul of soccer when considering alterations.

A close look at the reasoning behind the written rules provides three important clues to the interpretation of the Spirit of the Game in the form of three basic principles.

**EQUAL OPPORTUNITY.** All players must have an equal opportunity to demonstrate individual skills without unfair interference from opponents. Physical size or brute strength are not essential elements for success. Players of small stature can show their skills using quick reactions and balance alongside others whose assets include height and strength. Many players of small physique have achieved world fame by showing their exciting skills.

# THE SPIRIT OF THE GAME

**SAFETY.** Playing the game involves physical contact that can be tough. The rules provide a certain protection for players in specifying safety features for game components, equipment worn, and injury care, plus limitations to physical challenges for the ball.

**ENJOYMENT.** The rules are clear on describing unfair play and acts of misconduct that destroy skill and the pleasure of playing or watching the game. The purpose of the written rules is to provide a stimulating and healthy sport in which people of all ages can experience the maximum amount of enjoyment.

Summarizing then, the basic principles of the Spirit of the Game are simply: equality, safety, enjoyment.

The governing body for the Laws of the Game, the International Football Association Board, receives many suggestions to improve the game and change the laws. The following statement, issued by the IFAB after the annual meeting in 1968, remains valid in today's game: "It is the belief of the Board that the Spirit in which the Game is played is of paramount importance and that changes in the Laws, to improve the Game as a spectacle, are of little value if 'fair play' is not universally observed."

## FAIR PLAY IN SPORT

**DEFINITION.** Fair play in sport is a code of conduct that respects both the written and unwritten rules of play. Opponents are accepted as partners in sport.

Fair play is expressed through spontaneous actions that applaud sporting excellence, that show concern for opponents in distress, and that acknowledge defeat with dignity and victory with humility.

Sport with fair play enriches the quality of life.

# THE GAME OF SOCCER

Soccer (a contraction of Association Football) is a team game played by people of all ages. It is played for pure enjoyment in friendly games or competitively in matches between teams in organized tournaments.

**COMPONENTS** Essential components are players, a ball, and space.

**OBJECT** The object of the game is to combine the skills of the players in a team effort to move the ball through the opponents' goal to score a goal.

**MATCH RESULT** The team scoring the highest number of goals wins the match. If both teams score an equal number of goals, or if no goals are scored, the match is drawn.

**METHOD OF PLAY** To achieve a score, each team attacks the opponents' goal, generally by a series of passing movements of the ball, using any part of the body (except hands or arms) to put the ball through the goal. Each team has a goalkeeper who is allowed to use his hands to protect the goal.

**RULES OF PLAY** Matches are regulated by the Laws of the Game as decided by the International Football Association Board. These may be modified within approved limits for tournament play. Players are required to understand and respect the official Laws of the Game and any special tournament rules.

**THE REFEREE** To ensure that matches are played in accordance with the Laws and tournament rules, a Referee is appointed to supervise the play inside the field. Assistant Referees, when available, supervise certain aspects of play from outside of the field boundary lines.

**DECISIONS OF THE REFEREE** The decisions of the Referee regarding facts connected with play are final.

# DEFINITION OF TERMS USED IN THE LAWS OF THE GAME

**ADVANTAGE** When an offense occurs, the Referee may allow play to continue if it is to the advantage of the nonoffending team.

**CAUTION** A formal warning against further unfair play or unsporting behavior. Indicated by a yellow card shown by the Referee.

**COACH** A team official who may convey tactical instructions to the players during a match.

**DANGEROUS PLAY** Any action considered by the Referee to be dangerous to another player that is not a listed offense.

**FREE KICK** "The privilege of Kicking the Ball, without obstruction, in such a manner as the Kicker may see fit." (Original definition from 1863, which remains valid in the modern game.)

**GOALKEEPER** An identified player from each team permitted to touch the ball with his hands while inside the penalty area to defend the goal.

**HANDLING** Deliberate use of the hand or arm to influence the movement of the ball by a player other than a goalkeeper.

**IMPEDING** An offense when a player who is not playing the ball impedes the progress of an opponent by interposing his body between the opponent and the ball.

**MISCONDUCT** Any act of misbehavior contrary to the letter and spirit of the Laws of the Game.

**OFFSIDE POSITION** A player is in an offside position if he is nearer to his opponents' goal line than the ball, unless he (a) is in his own half, or (b) is level with the second-to-last opponent, or (c) is level with the last two opponents. It is not an offense to be in an offside position.

**OFFSIDE** An offense when a player is in an offside position and is judged, by the Referee, to be interfering with the play, with an opponent, or gaining an advantage.

**SCORING** A team scores a goal when the ball passes through the opposing team's goal in compliance with the Laws.

**TACKLING** A challenge made with the foot, either from the front or the side, to play the ball while it is in the possession of an opponent.

# COMPONENTS
## FOUR ESSENTIAL ELEMENTS
## TO START ANY MATCH

# COMPONENTS

A game of soccer does not need elaborate equipment. In kick-about games it is not even necessary to have a ball! Many children make do with objects varying from bundles of rags tied with string, cartons, and cans to paper cups, shoes, and caps.

What imagination! And what fun! No need for rules in these games. The playing area is any available space, be it in the streets, on a beach, on a flat roof, or inside a home.

The formal Laws of the Game are for soccer players who want to play in friendly team games or in organized matches in competitions.

Much care has been devoted to setting down the basic components common to all matches, no matter where they are played.

Standard equipment is intended to minimize elements of danger and encourage maximum effort.

The first four laws detail the essentials: the field of play, the ball, the players, and their equipment.

# LAW 1

## THE FIELD OF PLAY

- Soccer is played on a rectangular field to encourage the flow of play between the main targets, i.e., the goals.

- The size of the field may be varied between given limits according to the space available. However, the named areas within the boundaries are of fixed dimensions.

- The field is divided into two equal halves.

- Goal nets are advisable but not compulsory.

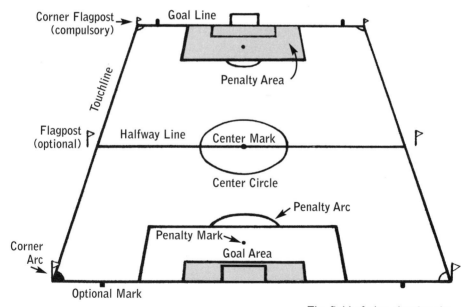

The field of play, showing the penalty, goal, and corner areas shaded.

- The size of the goal is related to the physical capability of the goalkeeper to defend the goal and to demand skill from attacking players to score.

- The goalposts are white in color so they can be seen easily.

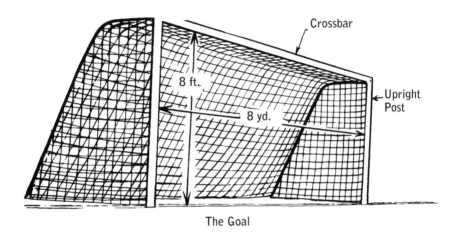

Crossbar

8 ft.

8 yd.

Upright Post

The Goal

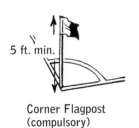

Corner Flagpost
(compulsory)

5 ft. min.

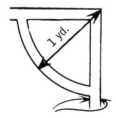

1 yd.

Corner Arc
2½–3 inch line
width advised
(up to 5 inches
allowed)

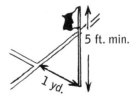

5 ft. min.

1 yd.

Halfway Flagpost
(optional)

**Line Markings**

# LAW 1

## THE FIELD OF PLAY

**Q** If, during a game, a crossbar is broken, may it be replaced?

**A** The use of a rope to replace the crossbar is not permitted.

- Flagposts shorter than five feet (1.50 m.) are dangerous.

# LAW 2

## THE BALL

- A spherical ball is chosen for the game of soccer because it truly reflects the skill of the player in kicking, heading, controlling, or moving it in any manner permitted by the rules.

- The size, weight, pressure, and materials used to manufacture balls are required to meet rigid FIFA standards.

**Q** Are all matches played with the same size ball?

**A** No. A smaller ball is advised for players under 16 years of age and for young women players.

**Q** May the ball be changed during a game?

**A** The ball may not be changed during the match without the authority of the Referee.

## Advice

It is advisable to choose a match ball inflated to suit the conditions of play. Generally, a soft ball is preferred on a hard surface and a harder ball on a soft or very wet surface.

# LAW 3

## THE PLAYERS

- In every match, there are two teams, each having not more than 11 players on the field. Where competition rules permit, up to three substitutes may be used. In noncompetition games, the teams agree on a maximum number.

- One player from each team is designated as a goalkeeper with the privilege of handling the ball within his team's penalty area.

**Q** A team starts a match with only 10 players. The 11th player arrives at the commencement of the second half. May he join his team?

**A** Yes, provided that the Referee is advised. If the game is in progress, the player must wait for a signal from the Referee.

A match may not start if either team consists of fewer than seven players.

**Q** May a player who has had to leave the field for treatment of an injury return to his team?

**A** Yes, after receiving a signal from the Referee.

**Q** A goalkeeper is injured and wishes to change places with another player. Is this permitted?

**A** Yes, at any time, provided that the Referee is advised when the change is to be made and that play has been stopped.

# LAW 3

## THE PLAYERS

**Q** What is the procedure for a substitute to join the game?

**A**

- There is normal stoppage of play.
- The Referee is notified.
- The outgoing player has left the field.
- The Referee signals the new player to enter the field.
- The new player enters at the halfway line.

**Q** If a player is dismissed from the game for misconduct, may his place be taken by a substitute (No. 12)?

**A** A player who has been dismissed **after** a match has started cannot be replaced.

A player who has been sent off **before** the kickoff may be replaced only by one of the named substitutes.

# LAW 4

## THE PLAYERS' EQUIPMENT

- The main points of this law are safety for the players and correct presentation on the field of play.

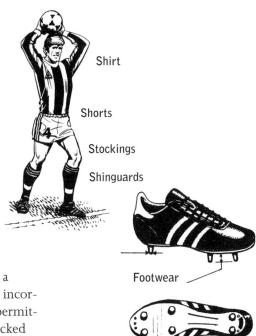

Shirt

Shorts

Stockings

Shinguards

- The basic compulsory equipment includes shinguards to protect the player's legs. In addition, it is the player's responsibility not to wear anything that could be dangerous to himself or to any other player. To assist players in obtaining a secure foothold, footwear incorporating bars or studs is permitted but these must be checked regularly to minimize the element of danger to other players.

Footwear

- Goalkeepers must be clearly identified by wearing colors that avoid possible confusion with other players, the Referee, and Assistant Referees.

**Q** Can any action be taken if a player advises the Referee that an injury has been caused by the studs on an opponent's boot?

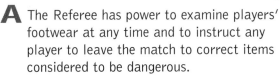

**A** The Referee has power to examine players' footwear at any time and to instruct any player to leave the match to correct items considered to be dangerous.

11

# LAW 4

## THE PLAYERS' EQUIPMENT

- The Referee may require a player to remove a ring or any other article that could cause injury.

**Q** May a player wear glasses during a match?

**A** The Laws do not prohibit glasses , face masks, or other protective equipment. The Referee must inspect such items to assess the potential danger to players.

**Q** A player decides to play without any footwear. Is this permitted?

**A** No. Compulsory equipment includes footwear.

**Q** When a player has had to leave the field to correct some item of equipment, how may he rejoin the game?

**A** The player must wait for a stoppage in the game before reporting to the Referee, who will then examine the player's equipment and satisfy himself that it is in order.

**Q** What would happen if a player who has left the field with the Referee's permission to correct dangerous equipment rejoined the game without waiting for play to be stopped?

**A** The Referee is required to caution the player. An indirect free kick is awarded to the opposing team.

# RULES OF PLAY
## BASIC PROCEDURES

# RULES OF PLAY

Now that we have the essential components,
the game can begin.

As with any other sport, the rules of play for
soccer deal with the method of playing the game—
how to start and restart, timing, how to score, etc.

Nine of the official laws deal with these
rules of play.

# LAW 7

## THE DURATION OF THE MATCH

- The normal period of play is 90 minutes, made up of two equal periods of 45 minutes. These periods may be slightly reduced for young players. Where competition rules allow, extra time may be played in the event of there being no result at the end of the normal period.

- When the game is delayed to allow an injured player to be examined or removed from the field, the Referee will make allowances to compensate for the amount of time lost.

- The Referee is required to make allowances for time lost during substitutions, dealing with offending players, or any other reason at the Referee's discretion.

**Q** As the Referee is about to signal the end of play, a defender handles the ball in his own penalty area. What action must the Referee take?

**A** A penalty kick must be awarded.

The Referee has authority to extend playing time to allow a penalty kick to be taken at the end of a normal period.

### Note

If a defender denies an opponent an obvious goal opportunity (as here) the Referee is required, by Law 12, to dismiss the offending player.

**Q** At the end of the first period of play, the visiting team's captain asks the Referee to commence the second period without an interval so that his team can start their return journey as early as possible. Would this be in order?

**A** The law entitles players to an interval at halftime not to exceed 15 minutes. There is no minimum. If all players agree to a brief interval, the Referee is allowed to consent unless a competition rule insists on a minimum period.

# LAW 8

## STARTING AND RESTARTING PLAY

- Each team defends one half of the field. The toss of a coin decides which team chooses the goal it wishes to attack. The other team will have first possession of the ball at the kickoff.

- After the halftime interval, the teams change ends. The second period of the match is started by a kickoff taken by the team that did not start play in the first period.

- Play is also restarted with a kickoff after a goal has been scored.

- To restart play after a temporary halt for any cause not mentioned elsewhere in the Laws, the Referee will drop the ball at the appropriate place.

**Q** Where should players stand at the kickoff?

**A** Every player is in his own half of the field. Players of the team opposing the kickoff remain not less than 10 yards from the ball until it is kicked and moves forward.

**Q** At a kickoff, the ball is kicked directly into the opponents' goal. Is this a goal?

**A** Yes. A goal may be scored directly from a kickoff.

**Q** May a player kick the ball before it touches the ground when it is being dropped by the Referee?

**A** No. The ball is not in play until it touches the ground. In this case, the Referee would drop the ball again.

# LAW 9

## BALL IN AND OUT OF PLAY

- The boundary lines, i.e. goal lines and touchlines, contain the game within a reasonable area to encourage the flow of play between the goal targets.

- The ball is out of play, and the game brought to a halt, when the whole of the ball has crossed over a boundary line, either on the ground or in the air.

- The lines belong to the areas for which they are the boundaries.

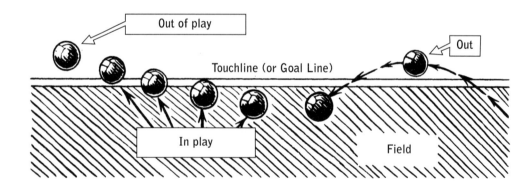

Out of play

Touchline (or Goal Line)

Out

In play

Field

# LAW 9

**Q** Should play be stopped if the ball strikes the Referee?

**A** No. Law 9 states that the ball is in play if "it rebounds from either the Referee or an Assistant Referee when they are on the field of play."

In the case shown here, a goal would be awarded.

**Q** If the ball goes over the goal line but is caught by the goalkeeper who is standing in the field of play, must the game be stopped?

**A** Yes, if the ball has passed completely over the goal line. The position of the goalkeeper does not alter this fact.

# LAW 10

## METHOD OF SCORING

- The team scoring the greater number of goals during a match is the winner. If both teams score an equal number of goals, or if no goals are scored, the match is drawn.

- To score a goal, the whole of the ball must pass over the goal line, between the posts, and under the crossbar.

- If the ball wholly crosses the goal line but returns into the field of play, the goal is valid.

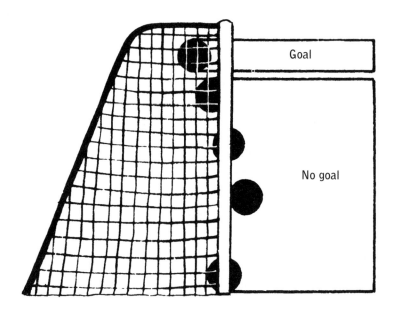

Goal

No goal

**Q** If the ball is about to enter the goal but is deflected by a dog (or spectator), can the Referee award a goal?

**A** The laws do not refer to this eventuality, but the traditional interpretation (in accordance with the spirit of the law) is not to allow a goal and to restart play by dropping the ball.

**Q** Would a goal be scored if a goalkeeper, standing in his own penalty area, throws the ball with the aid of a strong wind into his opponents' goal without any other player touching the ball?

**A** Yes. This is the only way in which an attacking player can score by the use of the hands.

# LAW 13

## FREE KICKS

- Free kicks are awarded by the Referee to penalize infringements of the Laws. "Free" means "free from interference by players of the offending team." They must not approach nearer to the ball than the limits imposed in the Laws until the ball has been kicked into play.

- There are two types of free kick:

(a) Direct—from which a goal can be scored against the opposing team when the ball passes directly into the goal;

(b) Indirect—from which a goal can only be scored if the ball is touched or played by a player of either team after it is kicked into play and before it enters the goal.

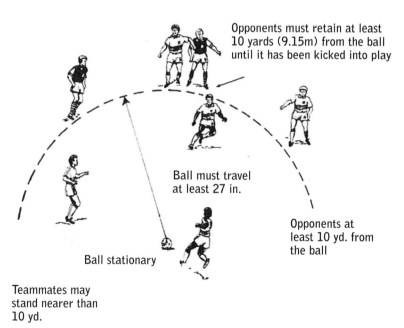

Opponents must retain at least 10 yards (9.15m) from the ball until it has been kicked into play

Ball must travel at least 27 in.

Opponents at least 10 yd. from the ball

Ball stationary

Teammates may stand nearer than 10 yd.

**Position of Players at a Free Kick**

**Q** If a defending player takes a direct free kick from outside his penalty area and kicks the ball past his own goalkeeper into the goal, what would be the correct decision?

**A** The Referee would award a corner kick to the attacking team because a goal can only be scored against the offending team from a direct free kick.

**Q** How do players and spectators know if the free kick is direct or indirect?

**A** When the Referee awards an indirect free kick he signals it by raising his arm. This signal precedes the blowing of the whistle for the free kick to be taken; no such signal is given in the case of a direct free kick.

If the ball goes directly into the opponents' goal from an indirect free kick, a goal kick is awarded to the defending team.

# LAW 13

## FREE KICKS

**Q** May the defending players stand less than 10 yards from the ball at any time?

**A** Only when an indirect free kick is to be taken from a position less than 10 yards away from the goal. Defenders may stand on the goal line between the posts.

**Q** Can defending players move nearer than 10 yards when the signal is given?

**A** Not until the ball has been kicked into play.

### Note

During a free kick, the kicker must not touch the ball a second time before it has touched another player.

**Q** If the defending team is awarded a free kick outside of their own penalty area, may the ball be kicked to the goalkeeper?

**A** Yes, but if the goalkeeper touches the ball with his hands inside the penalty area, an indirect free kick (Law 12) is awarded to the opposing team.

**Q** From an indirect free kick the ball strikes the crossbar, hits the goalkeeper, and bounces over the goal line. Would this be a goal?

**A** Yes, because the ball was last played by a player other than the kicker before it entered the goal.

# LAW 14

## PENALTY KICKS

- A penalty kick is an important award to punish any of the 10 offenses listed in Law 12 (see Page 66) when committed by a player within his own team's penalty area.

- Law 14 describes the requirements for taking a penalty kick. These include restrictions on the conduct of the kicker, the goalkeeper, and the other players.

- Playing time may be extended to allow a penalty kick to be taken (Law 7). The Referee decides when the penalty kick has been completed.

- The players other than the kicker are located:
  - Inside the field of play
  - Outside the penalty area
  - Behind the penalty mark
  - At least 10 yards (9.15 m) from the penalty mark

- The goalkeeper stands on the goal line between the posts.

Behind the Penalty Mark

**Positions of Players at a Penalty Kick**

**Q** The Referee has given the signal for the penalty to be taken, but before the ball is kicked, a defender moves into the penalty area. What is the correct procedure?

**A** The Referee will not delay the kick. If a goal is scored, it will be allowed. If a goal is not scored, the kick must be retaken.

**Q** What would happen if a player of each team encroached into the penalty area or within 10 yards of the penalty mark before the ball was in play?

**A** The penalty kick would have to be retaken.

# LAW 14

## PENALTY KICKS

**Q** Is the goalkeeper allowed to move before the ball is kicked?

**A** Yes, along the goal line but not toward the ball.

**Q** Would a goal be allowed if the ball was to strike the crossbar or goalpost and return to the kicker, who then kicked it into the goal?

**A** A goal would not be allowed because the kicker must not play the ball a second time until it has been touched by another player. The Referee would award an indirect free kick against the kicker.

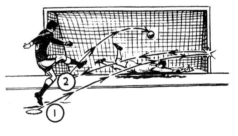

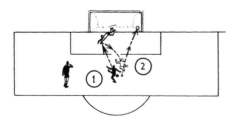

**Q** The Referee has extended time to allow a penalty kick to be taken. If the ball rebounds from the goalkeeper to the kicker who scores, will the goal be allowed?

**A** No. The game ends the moment the goalkeeper prevents the ball from entering the goal.

# LAW 15

## THROW-IN

- When the ball passes over a touchline, the game is restarted by a throw-in awarded to the team opposite to that of the player who last touched the ball.

- A goal cannot be scored directly from a throw-in.

Correct throw-in. Facing field of play. Both feet on ground. On or behind line.

Incorrect. Only one foot on ground.

Incorrect. Only one hand throwing ball.

Correct. Both hands throwing ball.

# LAW 15

## THROW-IN

**Q** Is this throw-in correct?

**A** Yes, provided that the ball
is thrown from behind and
over the head, and that
the action of throwing
is continuous from the
start of the throw to
the point of release.

**Q** A defender takes a throw-in
and throws the ball back to
his goalkeeper. The ball goes
directly into the goal before
the goalkeeper touches it. Is
it a goal?

**A** No. A goal cannot be scored
directly from a throw-in.
In this case, a corner kick
is awarded to the opposing
team.

# LAW 16

## GOAL KICK

- When a player of the attacking team plays the ball over the goal line, excluding the portion between the goalposts, the defending team is awarded a goal kick.

- The ball is not in play until it has been kicked directly out of the penalty area. A goal may be scored directly from a goal kick.

- The ball is kicked from any point within the goal area when all opponents are outside of the penalty area.

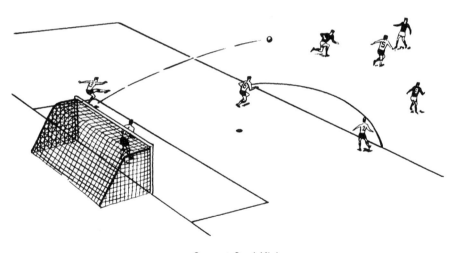

Correct Goal Kick

# LAW 16

## GOAL KICK

- If the ball is played before it passes outside of the penalty area, the goal kick is retaken.

**Q** If the ball is kicked over the goal line before it has cleared the penalty area, should the Referee award a corner kick?

**A** Because the ball was not in play when it crossed the goal line, the goal kick must be retaken.

# LAW 17

## CORNER KICK

- When a player of the defending team plays the ball over the goal line, excluding the portion between the goalposts, the attacking team is awarded a corner kick.

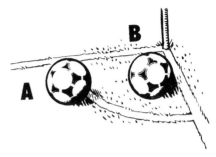

- The ball is placed inside the corner arc at the nearest corner flagpost. B is clearly inside the arc. A is acceptable because it overlaps the corner arc line.

**Ball Position in Corner Area**

**Q** Can the kicker move the corner flagpost?

**A** The corner area provides ample room for a player to take a corner kick. The flagpost must not be moved.

# LAW 17

## CORNER KICK

**Q** Which positions may attackers and defenders take in relation to the ball at a corner kick?

**A** Attackers may be as near to the ball as they wish, but defenders must be at least 10 yards away.

**Q** If the ball is kicked against a goalpost and returns to the kicker, may he then play it again?

**A** The kicker may not play the ball a second time until it has been touched by another player. An indirect free kick is awarded from where the ball was played for the second time by the kicker.

**Q** If the ball goes directly into goal from a corner kick, would a goal be allowed?

**A** Yes.

**Q** If the ball swerves over the goal line but back into play, should the game continue?

**A** The moment the whole of the ball has crossed the goal line, it is out of play. The game would be stopped and a goal kick awarded to the defending team.

# OFFSIDE

## SIMPLY EXPLAINED
## AND ILLUSTRATED

# OFFSIDE

Soccer is a team game. The objective is to combine the skills of the players to move the ball through the opposing team's goal.

The principle of offside is important to this objective because it discourages any player from trying to gain an unfair advantage by being in advance of the ball, near to the goal, to score with the minimum effort.

Other team games, such as rugby, hockey, and water polo have an offside rule based on the same principle—that a player caught in front of the ball is considered out of play, off-the-side, offside. The player must not try to interfere or influence the play in any way.

The offside rule demands alertness and intelligence from all players to assess tactical movements and devise countermeasures.

The offside rule contributes much to the attractive fluidity of a soccer game and to the pleasure of those who play or watch.

# LAW 11

## OFFSIDE

- This law is designed to discourage uninteresting play by attacking players. The game could be played without Law 11, but it could lead to players standing close to goal waiting for the ball for short-range attempts at scoring. Such play would require little skill or ability.

- It is not a difficult law to understand if two basic points are clearly established. They are:

(a) A matter of FACT based on the actual position of the player **at the moment the ball is played** by one of his own side;

(b) A matter of OPINION judged by his influence on the play and his motive for being in that position.

### Fact

A player is in an **offside position** when he is nearer to his opponents' goal line than both the ball and the second-to-last opponent.

**OFFSIDE EXAMPLES**

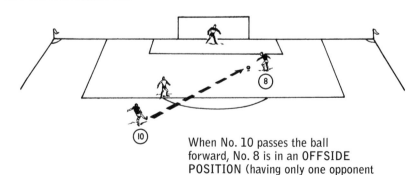

When No. 10 passes the ball forward, No. 8 is in an OFFSIDE POSITION (having only one opponent between himself and the goal line). He is clearly involved in active play and is adjudged OFFSIDE.

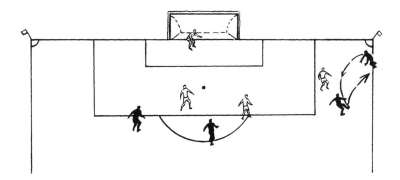

The ball is thrown in and immediately played back to the thrower, who is now OFFSIDE, being in front of the ball and having only one opponent between himself and the goal line.

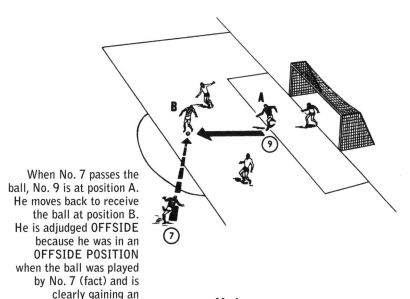

When No. 7 passes the ball, No. 9 is at position A. He moves back to receive the ball at position B. He is adjudged OFFSIDE because he was in an OFFSIDE POSITION when the ball was played by No. 7 (fact) and is clearly gaining an advantage by being in that position (OPINION).

## Note

When the ball is played by a teammate, a player cannot put himself on-side by moving back from an **offside position**.

# LAW 11

## OFFSIDE

No. 6 kicks the ball toward
the goal but it is deflected by
an opponent to No. 9, who
scores. The goal is not allowed
because No. 9 was in an
OFFSIDE POSITION and
involved in active play at the
moment the ball was kicked
by No. 6. The deflection by
the opponent in this case does
not affect the basic principles
of OFFSIDE.

No. 8 shoots for goal. The ball rebounds
from the crossbar to No. 11, who puts
it into the goal. The goal is not valid
because although No. 11 was behind
the ball when it hit the crossbar, he
was in an OFFSIDE POSITION
(having only one opponent
nearer to the goal line)
and gained an
advantage from
that position.

## NOT OFFSIDE

At the moment the ball is played toward
No. 11, he is not in an offside position
because he is level, or in line, with the two
last opponents.

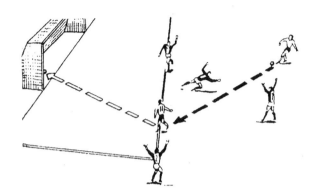

A player cannot be offside within his
own half of the field of play. In this case
the attacker has run forward into the
opponents' half after the ball was played.

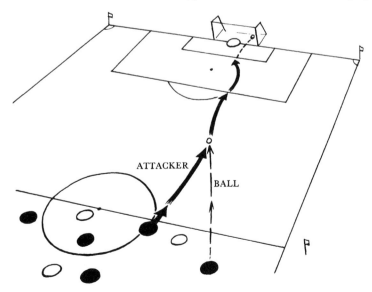

ATTACKER

BALL

# LAW 11

## NOT OFFSIDE

No. 9 is not offside because he was not in front of the ball when it was last played by a teammate.

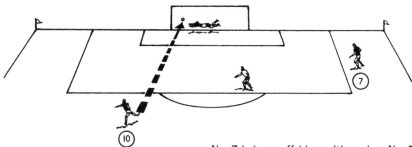

No. 7 is in an offside position when No. 10 kicks the ball into the goal. The goal is valid because No. 7 was not involved in active play.

No. 7 has moved on to the ball from a
forward pass. He was not in front of
the ball when it was kicked by
his teammate and is therefore
not offside.

A player cannot be offside if he
receives the ball directly from a
corner kick, a goal kick, or a throw-in.

# LAW 11

## NOT OFFSIDE

A player cannot be offside if he
receives the ball from a throw-in.
The goal is allowed.

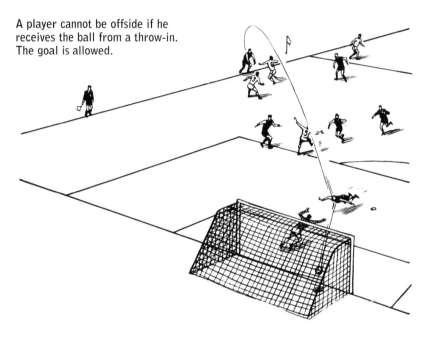

- Summarizing the Offside Law: In every possible situation only two questions need answering:

(i) Is the player in an **offside position** when the ball is played by one of his own side? (This is a matter of FACT.)

If the answer is yes, then,

(ii) Is he interfering with play or an opponent, or gaining an advantage? (This is a matter of OPINION.)

# FOULS AND MISCONDUCT

## WHAT NOT TO DO — OFFENSES AND PUNISHMENTS

# FOULS AND MISCONDUCT

At first sight, Law 12—Fouls and Misconduct—makes for gloomy reading because it is concerned solely with punishing players. However, on reflection, it is at the heart of the game.

The three basic principles of the Spirit of the Game are clearly exposed in this law.

**Equal opportunity** for all players to demonstrate their skills is provided by severely restricting the degree of physical challenges for possession of the ball. Playing fairly requires players to avoid challenges that are careless, reckless, or involve excessive force.

**Safety** is evident in protecting players from dangerous play.

**Enjoyment** is achieved by defining actions that are unacceptable in a healthy, fair, and exciting sport.

Law 12 comprises three parts:

(I) Major Offenses—direct free kick award

(II) Other Offenses—indirect free kick award

(III) Misconduct Offenses—caution or dismissal

# LAW 12

## FOULS AND MISCONDUCT

### (I) MAJOR OFFENSES

- Ten offenses are penalized by the award of a direct free kick to the opposing team. Nine relate to physical acts against opponents, the tenth being illegally handling the ball.

- A penalty kick is awarded if a player commits any of these offenses inside his own penalty area.

### EXAMPLES OF MAJOR OFFENSES

Tripping using the legs

Kicking an opponent

Tripping by stooping in front of
(or behind) an opponent

Jumping at an opponent
(The offending player
clearly has no intention of
playing the ball.)

Charging in a violent or dangerous manner

# LAW 12

## FOULS AND MISCONDUCT

A charge in the back can cause serious injury.

Attempting to strike an opponent will be punished as if contact had been made.

A goalkeeper who intentionally throws the ball at an opponent is guilty of striking.

# LAW 12

Holding with the
hand or arm

Pulling an
opponent's shirt is
a holding offense.

Pushing an opponent

# LAW 12

## FOULS AND MISCONDUCT

- Offense: deliberate handling of the ball with any part of the hand or arm.

- Exception: does not apply to the goalkeeper handling the ball within his own penalty area.

- Offense: a foul tackle from behind, contact made with opponent before touching the ball. May be a cautionable or dismissal offense depending on the severity of contact.

- Offense: kicking an opponent. This illustrates a "foot over" tackle, often interpreted as "serious foul play" requiring dismissal of the offending player.

- **Fair Charge**
  When trying to obtain possession of the ball, it is fair to
  attempt to put an opponent
  off balance without using
  excessive force. Here is an
  example of a fair charge:
  shoulder to shoulder, arms
  and elbows close to the body,
  ball within playing distance.

- **Unintentional Handling**
  An example of unintentional
  handling where the ball is
  kicked onto the hand. This is not
  an offense.

59

# LAW 12

## FOULS AND MISCONDUCT

### (II) OTHER OFFENSES

- Eight offenses are penalized by the award of an **indirect free kick** to the opposing team. Four of these are directed to the goalkeeper with the main intention to release the ball into play with minimum delay.

- The first three offenses are:

(a) Playing in a dangerous manner

(b) Impeding the progress of an opponent

(c) Preventing the goalkeeper from releasing the ball from his hands

### EXAMPLES OF OTHER OFFENSES

**(a) Playing in a dangerous manner**

Attempting to kick a ball near the head of an opponent is dangerous.

An overhead "bicycle" kick or a "scissor" kick (shown here) may be interpreted as dangerous play if attempted near other players.

## (b) Impeding the progress of an opponent

- Opponents are entitled to make a fair challenge for possession of the ball. When not playing the ball, it is an offense to impede (obstruct/block) an opponent by running between the opponent and the ball or interposing the body to block a challenge.

Even though the charge may be fair, the ball is not within playing distance and the opponent is impeded from getting to it.

# LAW 12

## FOULS AND MISCONDUCT

Running between an opponent and the ball is an example
of impeding, or obstructing.

This example of "screening" the ball
from an opponent is not "impeding"
because the ball is being played.

Obstruction is penalized when a player
blocks the opponent's path to the ball when
it is not within playing distance.

**(c) Preventing the goalkeeper from releasing the ball from his hands**

The goalkeeper is encouraged to release the ball from his hands and into play as soon as possible. It is an offense to prevent this by blocking his path.

### Goalkeepers: Restrictions on possession of the ball

- The role of the goalkeeper is to prevent the ball from passing through the goal. For this purpose, the goalkeeper has the special privilege of touching the ball with the hands inside the penalty area. To discourage abuses, and with the object of making the ball available to the other players with the minimum of delay, Law 12 lists four offenses specifically addressed to goalkeepers. They relate to excessive possession of the ball and restrictions on using the hands.

- Use of the hands is not permitted from a direct pass or from a throw-in from a teammate. To avoid the risk of being penalized for wasting time, goalkeepers are advised to release the ball within six seconds.

# LAW 12

## FOULS AND MISCONDUCT

Possession by goalkeeper

- The goalkeeper is allowed no more than six seconds when controlling the ball with the hands before releasing it. After releasing the ball, the goalkeeper is not allowed to touch it again with his hands until it has been played by another player. He may, however, play the ball with his feet.

- Goalkeepers are not permitted to touch the ball with the hands from a throw-in taken by a teammate. An indirect free kick is awarded where the offense occurred.

**Q** A goalkeeper falls on the ball and makes no attempt to release it until an opponent has retreated. Is this in order?

**A** No. The ball must be released within six seconds.

## (III) MISCONDUCT OFFENSES

- Any player who disregards the principles of the Laws of the Game by acts of discourtesy toward officials, persistence in committing offenses, or conduct that offends the accepted code of fair play in sport receives an official Caution from the Referee. This is a warning not to repeat unsporting behavior.

- For offenses of serious foul play; violent conduct; offensive, insulting, or abusive language; or repeated misconduct after receiving a Caution; players are dismissed from a match. Other offenses in this category include spitting at an opponent or any other person and denying an obvious goal-scoring opportunity to an opponent.

- The serious offenses described in the previous paragraph are reported to the appropriate authority (competition, regional, or national association, etc.). Further disciplinary procedures may follow, involving periods of suspension from playing and, in some cases, payment of fines.

- The following examples illustrate some acts of misconduct that damage not only the individual reputations of the players concerned but also offend the true ideals of fair play.

Showing dissent, by word or action, from any decision given by the Referee. Caution for first offense.

# LAW 12

## FOULS AND MISCONDUCT

Distracting or attempting to distract an opponent by shouting.
Caution for unsporting behavior. Indirect kick to the opposing team.

Kicking the ball away from the place where the Referee indicates a
free kick is to be taken, showing dissent from the decision, or delaying
the restart of play. Caution for unsporting behavior.

Foul play during a stoppage in the game.
Dismissal from the game.

An attacking player moves toward the goal with a clear chance to score
but is tripped by a defender. In addition to awarding a penalty kick
(the offense occurs inside the penalty area), the Referee dismisses the
defender for denying an opponent an obvious goal-scoring opportunity.
(Law 12—Sending-off offenses, No. 5.)

# LAW 12

## FOULS AND MISCONDUCT

Misconduct to the Referee at any time, even if it occurs off the field of play,
is dealt with as if it occurred during the game.

Misconduct toward an Assistant Referee (or Fourth Official)
at any time before, during, or after a match. Caution or
dismissal according to the offense.

# PLAY TO THE WHISTLE
## WHAT MATCH OFFICIALS DO

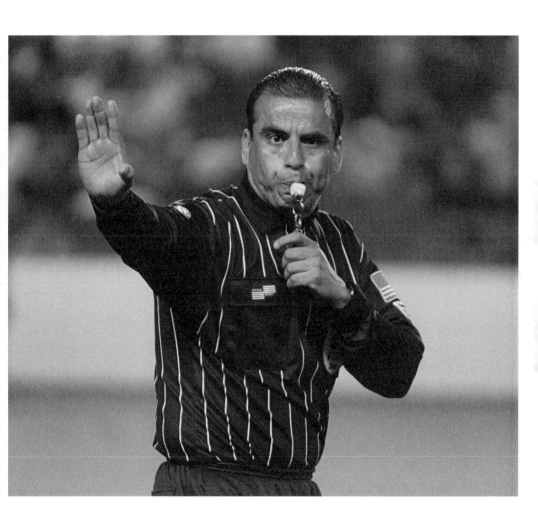

# PLAY TO THE WHISTLE

Match officials are not necessary in games played purely for fun, when the players control their own code of conduct and agree what is fair and unfair, just for the pleasure of kicking a ball among friends.

For organized matches, either as friendly games or in competitions, in which the teams agree to play according to the **Laws of the Game,** it is necessary to have a neutral person to decide points of contention and guide the conduct of the match within the rules.

Fully qualified **Referees** and **Assistant Referees** are trained experts in the interpretation and application of the laws.

The **Referee** is delegated many duties and responsibilities by match organizers. Effectively, the **Referee** is a superintendent appointed to manage, direct, and control a soccer match. Any issue that directly touches on the conduct of a match must be the concern of the **Referee** whether it occurs before, during, or after the event.

Section 5 outlines some of the tasks of the **Referee** and, when available, the **Assistant Referees.** It also includes a description of the method of match control employed by the officials—**The Diagonal System.**

Summarizing, an organized soccer match cannot be played to its full potential without the supervision of neutral officials. They apply the principles of the **Spirit of the Game,** ensuring that each player has an **equal opportunity** to demonstrate skills with concern for **safety** within the rules to aim for maximum **enjoyment.**

The decisions of the **Referee,** when relating to facts connected with play, are **final** even when they may be seen to be in error. The best advice for any player in doubt is to **Play to the Whistle.**

# LAW 5

## THE REFEREE

**The Referee**
**Usual Dress and Equipment**

- The Referee has the power to penalize when play has been stopped.

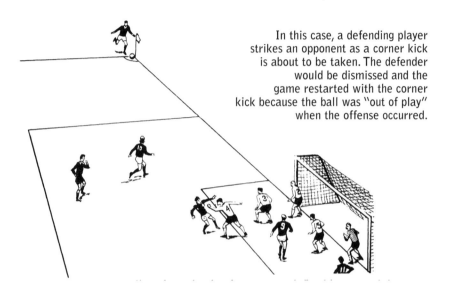

In this case, a defending player strikes an opponent as a corner kick is about to be taken. The defender would be dismissed and the game restarted with the corner kick because the ball was "out of play" when the offense occurred.

The attacking player (No. 8) is fouled, but the Referee has the power to refrain from stopping the play if it would be to the advantage of the offended team to continue. However, if the advantage is not realized within a few seconds, the Referee can penalize the original offense.

# LAW 5

## THE REFEREE

A defending player attempts to prevent a goal being scored by deliberately handling the ball. If the ball enters the goal, the Referee will allow the goal and not award a penalty kick for the handling offense. If the ball does not enter the goal, the offending player is dismissed for denying opponents an obvious goal opportunity.

- The Referee has the power to stop the game if, in his opinion, a player is seriously injured.

- Any player bleeding from an injury must leave the field and will only be allowed to return when the bleeding has been stopped.

- No person, other than the players and Assistant Referees, may enter the field of play without the Referee's permission.

In the situation shown here, the team official may be warned and reported.

- To communicate the severity of a disciplinary sanction to the player concerned and to others, the Referee produces a card:

  Yellow card = Caution
  Red card = Dismissal from
  the match

# LAW 5

## THE REFEREE

### SIGNALS—BY THE REFEREE

**BY LAW** Only two signals are mandatory in the Laws of the Game:

- Indirect Free Kick—one arm raised above the head (b)

- Discipline Cards—display of a colored card to an offending player

(a) Play on Advantage

(c) Direct Free Kick (direction)

(b) Indirect Free Kick

(d) Penalty Kick

**APPROVED SIGNALS**
**Instruction to players:**

- Play on Advantage—the Referee observes an offense but decides to apply the advantage option and signals play to continue (a)

- Direct Free Kick—a hand and arm signal to indicate direction of free kick (c)

- Penalty Kick—pointing to the penalty mark (d)

- Other Approved Signals—pointing to the appropriate position for a throw-in, goal kick, corner kick, free kick

**INFORMATIVE (UNOFFICIAL)**

- Instinctive gestures communicating the nature of offenses, for example, handling the ball, pushing, etc. (e)/(f)

(e) Handling the Ball

(f) Pushing

# LAW 6

## ASSISTANT REFEREES

- Neutral Assistant Referees, when appointed, are selected from a panel of qualified referees. As their title suggests, they assist the Referee to control a match in accordance with his instruction and the Laws of the Game.

Here, an Assistant Referee reports an offense by an attacking player that he noticed immediately prior to the scoring of a goal. The Referee, if he has not observed the incident, may act on the advice and cancel the goal.

If the ball strikes an Assistant Referee and is deflected over a boundary line, the game is restarted with a throw-in, goal kick, or corner kick. In this case, it would be a corner kick because a defending player last touched the ball and it was deflected over the goal line.

# LAW 6

## ASSISTANT REFEREES

### SIGNALS FOR THE INFORMATION OF THE REFEREE

- Flag signals indicate to the Referee when the ball goes out of play over a touch- or goal line and the correct decision, for example, goal kick, corner kick, or which side is entitled to a throw-in.

A special signal draws the Referee's attention to a request for substitution.

Substitution

Corner Kick

Throw-In Direction

Goal Kick

## SIGNALS—OFFSIDE

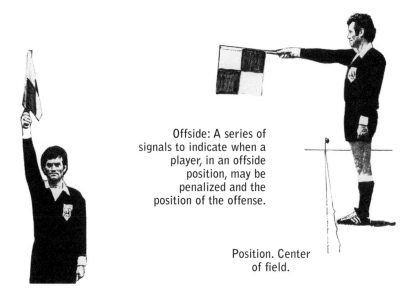

Offside: A series of signals to indicate when a player, in an offside position, may be penalized and the position of the offense.

Position. Center of field.

Offside. Flag in vertical position.

Position.
Far side.

Position. Near side.

# MATCH OFFICIALS

## THE DIAGONAL SYSTEM

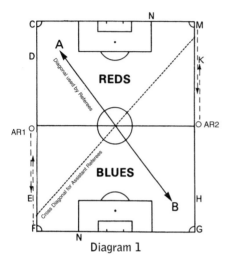

Diagram 1

- AR1 adopts the Reds as his side; AR2 adopts the Blues. As Red forwards move toward the Blue goal, AR1 keeps in line with the second-to-last defender. So, in actual practice, he will rarely get into the Reds' half of the field. Similarly, AR2 keeps in line with the second-to-last Red defender and will rarely get into the Blues' half.

- At corner kicks or penalty kicks, the Assistant in the half where the corner kick or penalty kick occurs positions himself at N, M, or F, according to the Referee's instructions. The Referee then takes position.

- The Diagonal System fails if AR2 gets between G and H when the Referee is at B, or when AR1 is near C or D when the Referee is at A, because there are two officials in the same place. This should be avoided.

- The imaginary diagonal used by the Referee is the line A-B.

- The opposite diagonal, used by the Assistant Referees AR1 and AR2, is adjusted to the position of the Referee.

- If the Referee is near A, AR2 will be at a point between M and K. When the Referee is at B, AR1 will be between E and F. This gives two officials control of the respective "danger zones," one at each side of the field.

## Note

Some Referees prefer to use the opposite diagonal, from F to M, in which case the Assistants adjust their patrol accordingly.

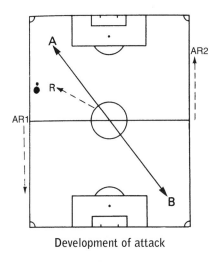

Development of attack

- Ball moves out to left wing. Referee (R) slightly off diagonal to be near play.

- Assistant Referee AR2 level with second-to-last defender.

- Two officials, therefore, up with play.

- AR1 in position for clearances and possible counterattack.

- Players ● and ○ line up for free kick.

- Referee (R) takes up his position just off his diagonal so that he is placed accurately to judge off-side. AR2 is more advanced but can watch for offside and fouls and also is in a good position to act as goal judge in the event of a direct shot being taken.

Free kick near goal
(just outside penalty area)

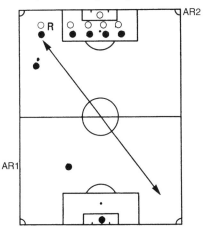

# SOCCER GUIDELINES

## GUIDELINES FOR
## THE SOCCER FAMILY

# THE FIFA FAIR PLAY CAMPAIGN

## CODE OF CONDUCT— 10 GOLDEN RULES

1  Play fair

2  Play to win but accept defeat with dignity

3  Observe the Laws of the Game

4  Respect opponents, team-mates, referees, officials, and spectators

5  Promote the interests of soccer

6  Honor those who defend soccer's good reputation

7  Reject corruption, drugs, racism, violence, gambling, and other dangers to our sport

8  Help others resist corrupting pressures

9  Denounce those who attempt to discredit our sport

10 Use soccer to make a better world

# PLAYER

You want to have fun and improve your
game. Knowing something about the rules
will add to your interest in soccer and help
avoid problems on the field.

## EQUIPMENT

Before every game, check your equipment for
any item that may prove to be dangerous to yourself or your opponents.
Footwear, in particular the studs you choose to suit the field surface condition, needs special care. The Referee may ask you to remove items of jewelry.

## STARTING PLAY

Remember the ball is not in play until kicked. The signal for the kick is
not the signal for you to move nearer than 10 yards to the ball.

## BALL OUT OF PLAY

The whole of the ball must be over the boundary lines before it is out of play.

## FREE KICK POSITION

Free kicks must be taken from the place where the offense occurred with
the ball stationary.

## 10 YARDS, PLEASE

Check what 10 yards means—for example, the center circle has a 10-yard
radius—and be at least this far away as soon as a free kick is awarded
against your team to avoid a yellow card.

## OFFSIDE

It's very important to understand this rule because your team loses a
chance to score and the ball is given to the opposing team every time you
are caught offside.

Study carefully the explanations and illustrations in Part 3. In particular,
realize that **offside** is first a matter of **fact**, i.e. **your position** in relation
to the ball and opposing players, and second a matter of the **opinion** of
the Referee as to **your involvement in active play**, and any advantage you
may gain by being in an offside position.

Offside position is judged at the moment the ball touches or is played by a teammate, not where you are when you receive the ball.

(a) You cannot be offside if you are behind the ball. If you are ahead of the ball, be aware of the positions of the opponents. Try to keep at least two players between you and their goal line.

(b) If you are in an offside position, get back behind the ball or avoid the next area of active play to convince the Referee that you are not influencing play or trying to gain an advantage.

(c) You cannot be offside if you receive the ball directly from a goal kick, a corner kick, or a throw-in.

## UNFAIR PLAY

You want to show your skills with the ball. So do opponents. Challenges for possession often involve hard physical contact. You will avoid being penalized if you control your challenges with care and by not being reckless or using excessive force.

## CHARGING AN OPPONENT

You may charge an opponent fairly, but not when the ball is out of playing distance or when you are making no attempt to play it.

## SPORTING BEHAVIOR

Nobody enjoys the spectacle of a player being cautioned or sent off. Study Law 12 to learn what actions are unacceptable and can be avoided.

## PENALTY KICKS

The important points to remember are:

(a) the positions of the players

(b) that players must remain at the proper distances until the ball is in play

(c) that the ball is in play when it has been kicked forward

# PLAYER

## THROW-IN POSITION

Throw-ins must be taken from the point where the ball crossed the touchline.

## GOALKEEPERS

Be aware of the following rules:

(a) Wear colors that distinguish you from other players and the Referee.

(b) The rules are strict about the amount of time that you are allowed possession of the ball and when you must not touch it with your hands.

(c) When you take the ball into your hands, you must release it into play without taking more than six seconds. If you exceed that time, you risk giving the opponents a free kick in a very dangerous position.

(d) Avoid any tactics that may be interpreted as wasting time.

(e) When challenged for the ball, avoid distracting opponents by shouting.

(f) You are not allowed to pull down the crossbar to prevent the ball from entering the goal. You will be cautioned.

(g) You will be penalized if you touch the ball with your hands when a teammate deliberately kicks it to you or throws it directly to you from a throw-in.

(h) Regarding item (c), understand that if you deliberately parry the ball with your hands, you are still considered to be in possession. Release the ball without touching it again with your hands.

(i) When facing a penalty kick, you may move along your goal line before the ball is kicked, but not from it—for example, advancing towards the ball. Also avoid any gestures that may be interpreted as attempts to distract the penalty kicker. This is unsporting behavior.

(j) If you intend on changing places with a teammate, be sure to advise the Referee in advance.

# REFEREE

You play a vital role in the amount of pleasure that people obtain from soccer.

Every game poses a variety of problems requiring instant and correct decisions. Only by clearly understanding the purpose and application of each Law can you carry out your duties efficiently. Some problems will arise that are not referred to specifically in the Laws. These must be solved with the application of common sense. Your feeling for what is fair and unfair will guide you to the right decision.

For qualified Referees, the following guidelines are intended as reminders of the basic duties and responsibilities you have been trained to accept.

For other members of the soccer family, a glance at the guidelines will give insight into the contribution of match officials to keep soccer a clean, healthy, and enjoyable family sport.

# REFEREE

## Section 1  COMPONENTS

**CHECKLIST**  Establish a routine method of checking all components by making a list of items to be examined. Your list should include the following:

(a) **FIELD**—condition of the playing surface, line markings, dimensions, inside areas, penalty and center marks.

(b) **GOALS**—safety of construction, anchorage, size, color, nets.

(c) **FLAGPOSTS**—positions, height, safety of construction.

(d) **BALL**—shape, size, pressure to suit game conditions, conformity with FIFA standards where necessary. Spare ball(s).

(e) **PLAYERS**—number on each team, substitutes, names, goalkeepers.

(f) **PLAYERS' EQUIPMENT**—colors, footwear, dangerous ornaments.

(g) **TIME**—complete checks to allow sufficient time to adjust incorrect items.

## Section 2  RULES OF PLAY

**COMPETITION RULES**  Check for any additions to or variations from the Laws that have been agreed to between the competing teams. In particular:

(a) **COMPONENTS**—for players under 16 years of age, women, and veteran players.

(b) **TIMING**—for players in item (a), periods of extra time. Allow for the time lost due to delays for substitutions, injuries, time-wasting tactics, and any other cause at your discretion. Players have a right to an interval at halftime not exceeding 15 minutes.

(c) **FREE KICKS**—Allow free kicks to be taken as quickly as possible so that the offending team does not gain an advantage by using delay to organize its defense.

(i) The ball must be stationary before the kick is taken.

(ii) Caution any player attempting to delay a free kick; for example, by moving the ball from its correct position.

(iii)Caution any player of the offending team who refuses to retire to the proper distance before the kick is taken.

(iv)At an indirect free kick, raise one arm before the signal to take the kick.

(d) **GOALS**—Do not award a goal unless you are sure that the ball has wholly crossed the goal line between the posts and under the crossbar.

(i) Check with your Assistant Referees before awarding a goal. A goal cannot be canceled after play has been restarted.

(ii) Keep a record of each goal as it is scored.

## Section 3   OFFSIDE

**BASICS** You have to first decide if the player is in an **offside position**. This is not an offense until you make a second decision based on your judgment of the player's influence on the play.

(a) **OFFSIDE POSITION**—Is the player in front of the ball in the opponents' half? If so, and if he is nearer to the goal line than the second-to-last opponent, the player is in an **offside position**.

(b) **OFFSIDE OFFENSE**—Is the player involved in the zone of play, for example by moving toward an opponent or the ball or gaining an advantage? If so, this is an **offside offense**.

(c) **MOMENT OF ASSESSMENT**—Offside decisions are assessed at the moment the ball touches or is played by a teammate.

# REFEREE

### Section 4  FOULS—MISCONDUCT

**FOUL PLAY**—Most foul play occurs when two players challenge for possession of the ball. Physical contact is inevitable in most instances and is an accepted part of the game. However, challenges must be kept under control, and to be fair, they must not be careless, reckless, or involve excessive force.

**DANGEROUS PLAY**—Attempting to play the ball may sometimes put an opponent in danger; for example, when the ball is close to the opponent's head or chest. An indirect free kick is the correct award.

**YOUNG AND WOMEN PLAYERS**—It is advisable to take special care in matches with young or women players to interpret physical challenges on the side of caution in order to reduce the risk of injuries.

**MISCONDUCT**—A policy of strict control over all forms of misconduct is recommended, not only to guide the particular match in your charge, but also to protect the overall image of the game. In particular:

(a) **UNSPORTING BEHAVIOR**—Attempts to gain an unfair advantage, contesting decisions, and disregard for the Laws of the Game form the general character of unsporting behavior in soccer. The purpose of cautioning players for any act under this heading is to reduce the need for more serious disciplinary action in subsequent play.

(b) **SERIOUS MISCONDUCT**—Any player who continues to behave in an unsporting manner after receiving a caution, who commits serious foul play, who behaves violently, who insults opponents or officials, or denies the opposing team a fair chance to score a goal, deserves the penalty of dismissal from a match and further punishment by the competent authorities.

(c) **PREVENTION**—A timely word of advice to players who appear to be losing self-control will help to complete the match without the necessity for severe disciplinary action.

## Section 5  PLAY TO THE WHISTLE

**MATCH CONTROL**—You may or may not have the aid of Assistant Referees to control your match. Whatever the situation, give careful thought to pregame conditions and how they may affect your method of control. You can form your opinion during the pregame check of the components listed in Section 1.

(a) **ADVANTAGE**—You have a few seconds of reflection to decide if a decision to allow advantage will have the desired effect. Do not hesitate to call back the play if it does not work. Also, do not allow an offender to escape a caution or dismissal (where appropriate) if it does work.

(b) **INJURED PLAYERS**—Stop the game immediately if a player appears to be seriously injured. You may save the player from long-term handicap, or worse. Do not wait for the players to kick the ball out of play—it is your duty to act quickly, particularly when a player has a head injury.

(c) **MEDICAL ASSISTANCE**—Find out before the game where you can call for aid should it be needed promptly.

(d) **SLIGHT INJURIES**—Wait for a normal stoppage to allow slightly injured players to leave the field for treatment. Where young or women players are involved, it is advisable to err on the side of discretion and stop play if in doubt.

(e) **SIMULATED INJURIES**—Be alert to players who pretend to be injured to gain an advantage—for example, delay—or to have an opponent disciplined.

**COACHING**—A team official is allowed to issue instructions to players during a match, provided that it is done in a responsible manner.

(a) **TECHNICAL AREA**—Check whether such an area exists at your match. If not, find out where the team officials will be located.

(b) **CONDUCT**—Be aware of any abuse of the coaching privilege and report any unsporting behavior to the competent authority.

# REFEREE

**ILLEGAL ENTRY INTO THE FIELD**—Do not allow officials or any other person onto the field of play without your permission.

**SIGNALS**—The Laws do not specify any code of signals apart from the raising of one arm to signify an indirect free kick. However, simple and discreet gestures, for example, touching a hand to indicate handball, will help you communicate with players and others and possibly reduce dissent.

# ASSISTANT REFEREE

Neutral Officials—You are a fully qualified Referee appointed to a match as an Assistant Referee. Prior to 1996, your title was Linesman. The new status recognized the importance of your task: assisting the match Referee in coping with increasing responsibilities. Apart from your basic duties listed in Law 6, the following guidelines will add to the effectiveness of your cooperation with the Referee. All are subject to instructions you receive from the Referee.

## COMPONENTS
Walk the field to check with the Referee. Bring any incorrect items to the Referee's attention.

## SUBSTITUTES
Assist with the checking of names, where they are located, and any special competition rules to be observed.

## TIMING OF PLAY
Time the play as if you are the Referee. Does the Referee need a signal to indicate time remaining?

## OFF-THE-BALL INCIDENTS
Any incidents of serious foul play, violent conduct, or any other misconduct that the Referee has not yet observed must be brought to his or her attention without delay.

# ASSISTANT REFEREE

## OFFSIDE
Know what the Referee wants in monitoring the play for offside situations, particularly at free kicks near the penalty area. Use field markings as references to judge zones of active play.

## COACHING
Draw the Referee's attention to any misconduct or movement outside of the technical area.

## IDENTIFICATION OF OFFENDERS
Make a note of players disciplined for misconduct to ensure correct identification in match reports.

## THIRD TEAM
The Referee and the two Assistant Referees form the "third team" at a match. The degree of cooperation you achieve will have an important bearing on the efficiency of control and the enjoyment of play.

# CLUB ASSISTANTS

Fully qualified neutral Assistant Referees may not be available. The two teams in a match are required, sometimes as a mandatory competition rule, to provide a person to act as a Club Assistant to the Referee.

## DUTIES
Both Club Assistants must report to the Referee before the start of the match for instructions as to the manner in which they can cooperate in the conduct of the match.

## GENERAL
The Referee usually asks for a signal to indicate that the ball has passed out of play over the touchline and which side is entitled to the throw-in. Other forms of assistance may be delegated, subject always to the fact that the Referee's decision is final.

# COACH/TEAM OFFICIAL

Your role in soccer was recognized in 1993 when the International Football Association Board agreed that you may convey tactical instructions to your players during the course of a match. This was an historical concession intended to "add to the quality of play."

It was granted on two main conditions:

(a) That you give your instructions from a specific location, a technical area when this can be provided, and

(b) That you behave in a responsible manner.

If a formally marked technical area is not provided, advise the Referee of the specific location from where you wish to give your instructions. You should remain in this location.

You are usually a person of much experience in soccer and have in your charge young players whose characters are forming at an impressionable age. Apart from the technical guidance you are qualified to impart in the playing of the game, you are a strong influence on the degree of respect your players show for fair play and their attitudes towards opponents, match officials, and spectators.

During a match, you are as emotionally involved as the players because you want to obtain a good result. However, in granting the concession of coaching during the play, the International Football Association Board expects you to accept the same criteria for correct behavior as is required of your players.

# ORGANIZERS

You may be a team manager, club official, competition organizer, or a volunteer giving your time so that others may share your affection for soccer.

For the correct organization of each match, the club has several duties and responsibilities. The following notes outline the main points.

**COMPETITIONS**—Clubs agree to comply with the rules of competitions, which may vary in some respects from the Laws of the Game (for example, in the number of substitutes, periods of play, extra time, etc.). It is the duty of the club to know both the Laws and agreed variations.

**MATCH OFFICIALS**—The club in charge of match arrangements is responsible for the welfare of the match officials before, during, and after the match.

**CLUB DISCIPLINE**—Each club is responsible for the proper conduct of its players and officials.

**MATCH ARRANGEMENTS**—The club in charge is responsible for providing:

(a) A field of play, correctly marked in accordance with Law 1, together with proper goals and corner posts with flags. Goal nets are desirable but not compulsory.

(b) The match ball plus spare balls if possible.

(c) Suitable dressing and washing facilities for the players and match officials.

(d) Whenever possible, a suitable barrier between the playing field and spectators. Sufficient space to be allowed to avoid interference with play and the patrol of Assistant Referees.

(e) The match officials with full details of match location, time of kick-off, and any other relevant information.

**CONSULTATION**—Consult with the Referee on any matter that may affect the correct conduct of a match, for example, security when many spectators are expected.

# SUPPORTERS

You probably support a particular club and enjoy the soccer family atmosphere as you marvel at the skills of your favorite players. Your presence and encouragement stimulates players to play well.

You can help people continue to enjoy soccer in other ways. Here are some suggestions.

**FAIR PLAY**—Insist on fair play, not only from players of other teams but also from your own favorites.

**MATCH OFFICIALS**—Appreciate the task of the officials from the guidelines in this publication. They try to ensure that each match is played to the spirit as well as the letter of the rules. They are members of the soccer family and deserve your support.

**PLAYERS' SKILLS**—Exciting skills are part of the joy of soccer, whether shown by your own players or opponents. Applaud both.

**COMBAT NEGATIVE INFLUENCES**—The FIFA Campaign for Fair Play appeals to the whole soccer family to recognize and combat dangers to soccer. Support FIFA by denouncing anyone who discredits our sport through corruption, drugs, racism, or violence.

**OTHER SUPPORTERS**—Those who support opposing teams share your passion for the game. They, too, are members of the soccer family. Respect and salute them.

**TO ALL SUPPORTERS! HELP KEEP SOCCER A CLEAN, HEALTHY, AND EXCITING SPORT, DESERVING OF THE TITLE:**

# "The People's Game"

# LEGENDS OF THE GAME

## UNIQUE AND UNUSUAL APPLICATIONS OF THE LAWS OF SOCCER

Photo courtesy of AP Images

# LEGENDS OF THE GAME

These famous incidents and facts from throughout the history of soccer illustrate just how good Referees have to be at thinking on their feet!

# SITUATION 1

## THE MYSTERY OF THE MOVING GOALPOSTS

In May 1976, soccer's remarkable impact on the American sports public received a boost when a major international tournament—the American Bicentennial Cup—was played in several important cities. The full national teams of Brazil, Italy, and England competed as a build-up to the 1978 World Cup.

A fourth team representing the United States included international stars Pelé and Rodney Marsh plus homegrown talent Bob Rigby and Kyle Rote Jr.

During the Team America match with England a mysterious incident occurred. Bob Rigby, the American goalkeeper, was seen moving the goalposts while the ball was in his penalty area!

Goalposts are normally securely fixed into the ground, but the goals at the John F. Kennedy Stadium in Philadelphia were portable frameworks resting under their own weight on the soccer field. Although heavy, the goal had been displaced by about a yard behind the goal line when a player collided with a post.

The incident was over in seconds, but soccer fans who enjoy discussing game situations posed the question: "What would have been the correct decision if the ball had entered the American goal before the posts were restored to the correct position?"

Soccer law at that time did not insist that goal posts be fixed to the ground. Rather, they simply had to be "placed on the center of each goal line." Rigby's posts were not in the correct position, so a goal could not have been allowed.

If the Referee was certain that the ball would have entered the goal, he might have dropped the ball at the feet of an attacking player with a clear chance to score!

Apart from the problem of potential movement, portable goals can also be dangerous. Current soccer law now insists that goals be securely anchored to the ground.

# SITUATION 2

## WORLD CUP FINAL GOAL—OR WAS IT?

Tension and drama are basic ingredients in any exciting soccer game—and never more so than at the World Cup Final of 1966, when England met West Germany at Wembley Stadium in front of 97,000 roaring fans. Many millions also followed the match on television.

With only seconds left to play, England was set to win, 2–1. But Wolfgang Weber tied the score with a free kick, sliding the ball beyond the reach of goalkeeper Gordon Banks. The exhausted players faced 30 agonizing minutes of extra time. For the Germans, it was another chance to snatch the prize; for the English, it was a victory that had to be secured again.

Near the end of the first period of extra time, a controversial incident sealed the fate of the thrilling encounter. Highly dramatic at the time, the situation has since been debated for many years.

Alan Ball, England's compact and nonstop midfielder, centered the ball from the right touchline to Geoff Hurst. Hurst controlled it, turned, and crashed it toward the German goal. As illustrated, the ball struck the underside of the crossbar and deflected down to the goal line. It bounced out and was headed away by Weber.

The Swiss Referee, Gottfried Dienst, uncertain whether the ball had bounced on or behind the line, looked anxiously to his linesman, Russian Tofik Bakhramov. The linesman's flag was up. Dienst stopped the play and ran to the touchline for an animated consultation. Millions held their breath. The Referee turned and pointed firmly to the center of the field—a goal! Naturally, the English welcomed the decision; the Germans protested, but to no avail. Then, in the last seconds of extra time, Hurst scored another goal, his third, to give England a glorious victory, 4–2.

Exhaustive studies of photos, films, and computer analyses have never proved conclusively that the ball had wholly crossed the line for England's third goal. It remains a question mark in soccer history, but the result will never be changed because, in soccer law, the Referee's decision is final.

# SITUATION 3

## WITCHCRAFT IN SOCCER

According to some tales, Africa is a dark continent full of mysteries. Some even say that African soccer has a special ingredient: witchcraft that calls on powerful forces to influence the fortunes of teams and players. Such forces are described as muti, or medicine. Medicine can be good or bad, depending on who is giving or receiving it, as the following true stories show.

- Some fans carry a rabbit's foot or a goat's foot wrapped in cloth containing special herbs and animal substances to keep evil spirits away from their team. Such talismans are often found near a soccer field after a match.

- A team may refuse to play with a ball that has been touched by the manager of the opposing team because he may have put a magic spell on it to favor his own team.

- A goalkeeper who throws his cap into the back of his goal may be accused of putting an evil curse on the goal to prevent opponents from scoring.

- When the ball is kicked into the crowd, it may be knifed by a fan of the losing team to kill evil spirits.

- At one match, the teams were ready to start when a fan rushed to the center and placed an object under the ball. Knowing the teams would not play until the "spell" had been removed, the Referee chased and caught the offender. He led him back to the ball and ordered the players to stand clear while the fan lifted it to expose the dark secret: the cap of a Coke bottle!

Africans are not unique in calling on witchcraft or superstitions to help their cause. Many players from around the world have special charms for good luck or follow rituals such as touching a "lucky" object or person, wearing "lucky" boots, colors, numbers, etc.

When witchcraft is about, Referees need to have special knowledge and diplomacy to keep their heads—literally!

# SITUATION 4

## RELEGATION AFTER AN ILLEGAL GOAL

Soccer facts are often interesting, but limited in narrative value. For example, it is a fact that on April 2, 1952, Tottenham Hotspur beat Huddersfield Town 1–0 in the English First Division. Behind the fact lies a story that is recorded in soccer history because the result was directly influenced by an error in applying soccer law. The error changed Hudderfield's status as a First Division club; a few days later the club was relegated to the Second Division.

Tottenham won a corner kick late in the game. The illustration (opposite) shows the sequence of events. Baily, the Spurs outside-left, kicked the ball low and hard towards the Huddersfield goal. The Referee, Mr. Barnes, was struck by the ball and dazed for a few seconds. The next thing he saw was the ball headed into goal by Duquemin, Spurs center-forward. Mr. Barnes immediately awarded the goal and was surprised by the protests of Huddersfield players.

The protests were not unreasonable. What the Referee had not realized was that the ball had rebounded off of him to Baily and that Baily had kicked the ball again before Duquemin scored.

Soccer law does not allow a player who takes a corner kick to play the ball again until it has been touched by another player. The fact that the ball rebounded from the Referee is irrelevant. Mr. Barnes consulted a linesman but found no reason to cancel the goal.

After the match, Huddersfield filed a formal protest requesting that the match be declared void and asking for a replay. The Football League rejected the protest, as did a special court some weeks later. As a result, Huddersfield was denied another chance to avoid relegation.

This incident was a classic case of the Referee being right even when shown to be wrong!

The story has a happy sequel. Huddersfield Town won promotion back to the First Division the following season.

# SITUATION 5

## ONE SHOT, THREE MONTHS IN PRISON

Soccer match problems are not always created by the players. Take the case of Jean-Marc Luccheti, a fanatical supporter of the Corsican team Calenzana.

April 23, 1978, was a most important date for Jean-Marc. Calenzana was playing a vital relegation match against big rivals from Murato, near Bastia. Toward the end of a tense game, Calenzana was holding Murato to a draw to gain a valuable point. Suddenly, a Murato forward ran through the defense and kicked the ball toward an empty goal.

Jean-Marc, standing on the touchline, had given his team his usual vocal encouragement—but was it enough? The ball was surely going into the goal. It would be a catastrophe if Murato scored now.

Jean-Marc decided on swift action to save the day. Producing a gun from his pocket, he fired at the ball. His aim was true. The ball dropped instantly, with a final rush of air from its lifeless carcass, just short of the goal.

Jean-Marc must have known that soccer law does not allow a goal to be scored if interference from an "outside agent" prevents the ball from entering the goal. In the confusion that followed, the match was ended by the Referee, who declared he had neither seen nor heard anything unusual!

Calenzana had escaped defeat, but Jean-Marc was arrested and had to pay a price for his loyalty. He was sentenced to three months in prison for possessing an illegal weapon.

# TEST YOUR SOCCER IQ

## COMMON GAME SITUATIONS TO TEST
## YOUR SOCCER KNOWLEDGE

# TEST YOUR SOCCER IQ

You should now have a good basic knowledge of the game of soccer—how it should be played, the roles of the players, the coaches, the match officials, club organizers, administrators, supporters, and everyone else who contributes his or her expertise toward maintaining soccer as the world's number one sport. You should now understand the main points of the rules and how they guide play and are applied by the Referee. Added to your previous knowledge, understanding the Laws of the Game will help you to be aware of and appreciate the many facets of soccer.

This next section is intended to help you check your overall know-how of soccer—your soccer IQ. These illustrated game situations could arise at any time, and you'll need to know what's legal and what the correct action is in each situation.

See how your answers match with the solutions provided and determine your soccer IQ from the rating guide. Show the situations to your soccer friends and surprise them with your knowledge!

**WHEN NOTING YOUR ANSWERS, IDENTIFY THE OFFENSE AND THE ACTION REQUIRED (WHERE APPROPRIATE).**

1. A player stops the ball with the top of his arm. Is this allowed?

2. An indirect free kick is to be taken nearer than 10 yards from the goal. Defenders line up on the goal line between and outside the goalposts. Is this allowed?

3. A substitute does not wear the same color of shirt as his teammates. Can he play?

4. During a corner kick, an attacker positions himself in front of the goalkeeper. Is this allowed?

5. A player deliberately holds up play by taking the ball to the corner and shielding it from opponents. Is this allowed?

6. A goalkeeper inside the penalty area pushes an opponent with the ball. What is the correct decision?

7. A player plays the ball with a sliding tackle, causing an opponent to fall over his leg. What action should be taken?

8. A player, wearing a captain's armband, protests a decision. Is this allowed?

9. During a penalty kick, a defender obtains permission to leave the field and stands beside a goalpost and behind the goal line. Is this allowed?

10. During a throw-in, a player tries to distract the thrower. Is this permitted?

11. In the penalty area, a defender
    ignores the ball and jumps at
    an opponent. What is the correct
    decision?

12. Two players from the same team are fighting inside their own
    penalty area. The game is stopped, and the two players are dismissed.
    How is play restarted?

13. When a game is started, the ball is passed back to a teammate. Is this allowed?

14. During a free kick, defenders form a line 10 yards from the ball. Three attackers then position themselves between the ball and the defenders. Is this allowed?

15. Are players allowed to smoke during a match?

121

16. A player attempts to kick a knee-high ball as an opponent tries to head it. Which player should be penalized?

17. The Referee has stopped the first half two minutes too soon and the players are leaving the field. Should he recall the players or add two minutes to the second half?

18. A defender kicks the ball to his goalkeeper but an opponent, in an offside position, intercepts and scores. Is the goal allowed?

19. A goalkeeper shouts and distracts a teammate in order to obtain the ball. Is this allowed?

20. After 10 minutes of play, a Referee realizes that two players from the same team are wearing the same number. Which player should be dismissed?

123

21. If a player jumps at the ball with both feet when an opponent is in possession, is this considered dangerous play?

22. While the ball is in play, a player on the field uses offensive language toward his own coach. What is the correct action?

23. An attacker is unable to avoid the ball when it is kicked at his arm. It bounces to his advantage and he scores. Is the goal allowed?

24. A player disobeys a team instruction and is dismissed by his captain. Is this allowed?

25. The match is finished. A player strikes an opponent. Can any action be taken?

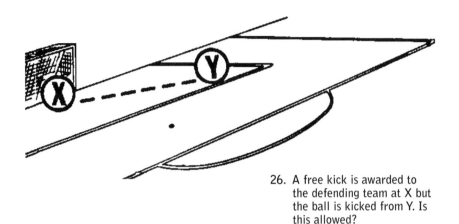

26. A free kick is awarded to the defending team at X but the ball is kicked from Y. Is this allowed?

27. A defender runs over the goal line to place player No. 8 in an offside position. The ball goes into the goal. What is the correct action?

28. The ball is trapped between the legs of the goalkeeper. May an opponent attempt to kick the ball?

29. Play is restarted by dropping the ball. It falls to an attacker in an offside position. He scores. What is the correct decision?

30. A Referee realizes that a scoring player is a substitute who has replaced a teammate during the half-time break without notifying the Referee. Is the goal allowed?

31. A player is instructed to remove objects that the Referee considers to be dangerous. The player refuses, saying they have religious significance. What should be done?

32. An injured player receives permission to leave the field for treatment. Later, he runs onto the field without permission from the Referee and kicks the ball into the goal. Is the goal allowed?

33. The Referee stops play when a player is seriously injured. A defender then strikes an opponent inside the penalty area. He is dismissed. How is the game restarted?

34. The attacking team's goalkeeper says he will take a penalty kick. Is this allowed?

35. After a free kick is taken, defenders rush forward to leave an opponent in an offside position. He scores. Is the goal allowed?

36. A goalkeeper makes a mark from the center of his goal to the goal area line. Is this allowed?

37. From a free kick, a player lifts the ball in one movement over a defensive wall. Is this allowed?

38. After catching the ball, the goalkeeper falls inside the arc that is added to the penalty area. What is the correct decision?

39. Is an attacker allowed to stand on the opponent's goal line when a free kick has been awarded to the defending team outside the penalty area?

40. The ball is going toward the goal line for a goal kick. A defender shields the ball from an opponent without attempting to play it. Is this allowed?

# ANSWERS

1. No. The ball must not be deliberately handled by any part of the arm. The correct award is a direct free kick or a penalty kick if the offense occurred in the offender's penalty area.

2. No. All defenders must be on the goal line and between, not outside, the goalposts.

3. Yes, provided that the colors do not cause confusion with opponents.

4. Yes, provided there is no attempt to impede the goal-keeper when the corner kick is taken.

5. Yes. The ball is in play and this is a legitimate tactic.

6. A penalty kick.

7. None. The ball was played. A sliding tackle is not an offense unless it endangers an opponent.

8. No. A team captain is not permitted to question a Referee's decision. He should be cautioned for unsporting conduct.

9. No. The defender should move away from the goal to avoid distracting the penalty kicker.

10. No. This is unsporting conduct and may draw a yellow card.

11. A penalty kick.

12. Play should be started with an indirect free kick.

13. No. The ball must be kicked forward. The kick-off is retaken.

14. Yes. There is no restriction on where the attackers may stand.

15. No.

16. The opponent, because the heading action is unfair on the kicker. An indirect free kick should be awarded.

17. The players should be recalled to complete the two minutes remaining in the first half.

18. Yes, because the attacker received the ball directly from an opponent.

19. Yes. Tactical calling is allowed provided that it is not intended to distract an opponent.

20. There is no offense. Soccer law does not require players to be numbered. If a competition rule requires numbers, the matter should be reported after the game.

21. Not unless there is any real danger to the opponent.

22. The player should be dismissed and the match restarted with an indirect free kick.

23. Yes, because the attacker did not handle the ball deliberately.

24. No. Only the Referee has the right to dismiss a player.

25. Yes. The offending player must be reported as if the incident occurred during play.

26. Yes. The ball may be placed anywhere within the goal area.

27. The goal is valid. The defender may be cautioned for leaving the field without permission.

28. No. This is dangerous play. The Referee should award an indirect free kick to the defenders.

29. A goal. A player cannot be offside from a dropped ball.

30. Yes. The substitute must be cautioned.

31. If the objects cannot be made safe, the player must not be allowed to play.

32. No. The player is cautioned and an indirect free kick awarded.

33. Play is restarted with a dropped ball where it was when the Referee stopped the game. The offense occurred when the ball was out of play.

34. Yes. Any player of the attacking team may take the kick.

35. Yes, because the attacker was not in an offside position when the ball was kicked into play.

36. No. The mark is an artificial aid. The goalkeeper may be cautioned.

37. Yes, provided that the ball is touched only once.

38. A direct free kick against the goalkeeper for handling the ball outside the penalty area.

39. Yes, because the free kick is outside the penalty area and the attacker is more than 10 yards from the ball.

40. Yes, because the ball is within playing distance of the defender.

# YOUR SOCCER IQ

For each completely correct answer, give yourself five points. For a partially correct answer, grade your score according to the degree of success—i.e. one, two, three, or four points. For example, if your answer to No. 28 is "no" but you have not said why or that an indirect free kick is awarded, give yourself two points. Score another point if you added dangerous play or the indirect free kick award.

### 200:
Soccer Expert. This should be the level for all Referees.

### 150-199:
Excellent. All experienced players should achieve at least a 150.

### 100-150:
A good basic level to build on for avid fans and young players.

### 50-100:
You are probably content just to follow the play and miss out on the whys and wherefores.

If you want to improve your soccer IQ, recheck the incorrect or incomplete answers to find your weaknesses in identifying the offense and/or the correct action. Reexamine the illustrated examples and look up the appropriate rules to learn more.